How to Explain a Diagnosis to a Child

An Interactive Resource Guide for Parents and Professionals

Authors: Janet Arnold, BA, RECE & Francine McLeod, BSW, RSW

This book is dedicated to all the wonderful individuals and families we have had the pleasure of working with over the years. You have influenced us in many ways and enriched our lives forever.
Thank you for teaching us!

Table of Contents

Foreword

I am more than pleased to introduce this wonderful resource guide by Janet Arnold and Francine McLeod. I have had the opportunity to know, and work with Janet in a professional capacity for many years, and I truly support the work she and Francine do every day to help better the lives of so many.

Their research greatly impacts the lives of not only children, but of families, educators and other professionals who support them towards becoming a successful adult. Janet and Francine have dedicated over 20 years to implementing evidence-based approaches, to meeting the needs of children, youth and young adults. This guide considers intervention strategies and innovative ideas that they themselves have used with others to help explain a diagnosis.

This much-needed resource truly captures the individual needs of each child, and allows families and professionals to take their time to help guide children through a difficult transition. Being able to understand what it means to have a disability can be overwhelming for many individuals. As parents, we want to be the role models for our children to teach them to be able to advocate and to embrace their disability, and know that all children have strengths and to be able to work from there. This insightful and practical book should be in the hands of all parents to ensure that their child is successful in embracing their diagnosis. It is of utmost importance for parents to reach out to community resources for support and encouragement, and to always remember that YOU are not alone in this journey.

This is an interactive step-by-step guide that allows you to consider the needs of your child while focusing and building on their strengths. Janet and Francine have included helpful hints to tailor the sessions further. Janet and Francine have taken a strength-focused approach with an overall positive message about a child's disability, being "That it is okay to be different, and that you are important". They truly have tried to capture "It's not what you say, it's how you say it."

I have thoroughly enjoyed reading this guide and know that the information inside will benefit so many. Thank you, Janet and Francine, for believing those with a disability, are just like you and me.

Lynn Ziraldo,
Strategic Advisor for LDAYR
Retired Executive Director of YRDSB after 38 years
Past President of Ontario and Canadian Council of Exceptional Children
Parent who has walked in your shoes for over 40 years

Authors' Notes

How to Explain a Diagnosis to a Child was written with 20 plus years of experience working with individuals who have been diagnosed with various disabilities/disorders. Parents and professionals have asked us for information as to how to explain a diagnosis to a child. We have used a variety of resources and consulted with psychologists in related fields to help us deliver this service to our clients. Most importantly, we have consulted with the parents of these children, and at times, gained insight from the individuals themselves. Thus, we have decided to take our experience and knowledge to create this interactive guide that provides parents with the tools to explain a diagnosis to a child by themselves, or in consultation with a professional. This guide provides step-by-step sessions that can be tailored to meet the needs of everyone.

We would like to offer our utmost sincere and heartfelt thanks to all the children and their families who we have had the pleasure of working with over the years. You have welcomed us into your homes, and allowed us to join you on this journey together.

We would also like to offer special thanks to all the professionals we have worked with over the years. You have provided us with insight and mentored us into continuing to grow our professional skills.

Lastly, we would like to thank our own families, who have continued to support our dreams, the work we do, and helped us believe that one day, this resource would be possible.

Personal Stories

Parent of a son with Attention Deficit Disorder (ADD) and a Learning Disability (LD)

Have you ever experienced "that feeling?" The one that just doesn't sit well. The feeling when you see your child struggling to learn something new, or behaving in a manner that causes those butterflies in your stomach. As a parent, you try to listen and believe the comments of others: "Don't worry, it's a boy thing!"; "Remember, he is a November baby"; "He just needs to learn to focus more"; or my all-time favourite: "I'm sure he will grow out of it." Despite their good-intentioned comments and attempts at reassurance, you know both in your head and in your heart, that something just isn't right. My suggestion is to trust your instincts! You are probably beginning to realize that your child is "different," and that something else is in fact going on.

This is my story. It is one of being a professional who has supported children with bright minds and varying abilities for the past 20 years, but also of a parent who has traveled an unexpected journey with her son. I am proud and happy to share my experiences with you, as you too may have traveled a similar road.

On November 23, 2004, my husband and I, alongside our family and friends welcomed the birth of our first beautiful baby boy, after a long and fairly typical delivery. Over the course of his growth and development, I am happy to say that he met all developmental milestones, excelled in speech and language development, and we, as new parents, enjoyed seeing him grow into a loving, happy, little boy. He demonstrated a love and passion for playing and interacting with others who were familiar to him.

As he transitioned from a toddler to an energetic preschooler, we enrolled him in a classroom environment to help prepare him and provide him with the necessary learning skills to get him ready for his early entry to Junior Kindergarten. The focus was primarily a hands-on play based approach, which served my son very well. He thrived in this environment, and we were more than happy with his progress. Then came the entry to Junior Kindergarten. Our son was enrolled in a small class that was comprised of just three boys (our son included), the rest being girls. I can honestly say this is where our lives took a shift, a detour in the road. There was increased emphasis on sitting for circle time, answering in front of the group, paper and pencil tasks, and a reduced opportunity for free play. We started to receive feedback from our son's teacher about his "behaviour" in the class. Our son was not "getting in trouble" for misbehaviour.

The nature of the feedback was that he didn't seem interested in learning, and that all he wanted to do was to play. As concerned parents, we took this feedback, and investigated further into the foods he was eating, and we enrolled him in extra-curricular activities to help with focus while still allowing him the opportunity to be active. Overall, he did well, learned some of the academic curriculum and was happy to transition to Senior Kindergarten.

Over the next few academic years, feedback from teachers was similar and always ended with: "Don't worry, he is still young for his grade," or "I'm sure with a little more focus he will improve." Comments like this only fueled my involvement, and increased the amount of teacher-parent interactions. With an increased involvement, I actively worked in partnership with my son's educators and tutors to help provide him with the necessary supports he needed to manage in the classroom. I cannot lie and say that I wasn't concerned about his academics, yet the main focus of my concern was on his self-confidence. This was an area that I highly stressed to my son's teachers, and wanted to ensure he never felt like he wasn't good or smart enough because I knew differently.

Over the course of his schooling, I became an advocate for my son, and despite what others may have said to me, I knew that in grade two a formal assessment was needed. In honesty, I was not shocked by the results, as I think I had known all along. My son's diagnosis with a Learning Disability and Attention Deficit Disorder only strengthened my commitment to work collaboratively with his educators to ensure his rights and needs as a student were being met.

My journey with my son has been filled with frustration, tears and laughter. I am a parent who like all, loves her child, believes in her child's ability and at times needs to fight for him to get the supports that are his rights. Our goal is for our son to advocate for himself, and hope that our voice, and his own voice will help pave the way for others who share a similar story. Our child, like your child has a bright mind and will lead a successful and happy life!

Parent of a son with Autism

Revealing to someone that they have autism is imperative. There was never any doubt in my mind that we should tell our son about his diagnosis. Making it meaningful to a 6-year-old, however, is challenging. When Jack was first diagnosed with autism, discussing his diagnosis with him was the furthest thing from our minds. He was non-verbal, and diagnosed as having moderate to severe autism. So, having any preconceived ideas about when we would discuss his diagnosis were futile at that time. However, as his communication skills developed, it became clear that this was a conversation that we really needed to have with him. He knew he was different because he only attended school half days and attended therapy for the remainder of the day. Jack had an awareness that psychologists, ABA therapists and the like were not an integral part of most 6-year old's lives'. He questioned why he needed to have therapy while the other kids stayed at school. So, for us, it was important to reveal to him how crucial therapy was to his development. It was best that he knew what his strengths and weaknesses were, so we could help him learn to function in our confusing and, for the most part, overwhelming world. I had heard of a family who decided not to tell their son about his diagnosis. When this child was 13 years old, he came to his parents and said that he thought something was really wrong with him. He was distressed at the fact that he was so different from his peers. When his parents told him of his diagnosis, this child was actually relieved. Many aspects of his life began to make sense. There was now a reason why he found it difficult to form and maintain friendships, for example. It also became easier for him to 'work around' his difficulties. I certainly did not want Jack to live life confused as to his identity. The neuro-typical world is already a very confusing place for those on the spectrum. We just wanted to shed light on one part of this convoluted world, in the hopes that it would be less confusing for our son. As Jack grows, his understanding of his diagnosis will too. Our hope is that it will only strengthen his resolve to adjust his daily life so that he can continue to grow and develop.

Caylin, young adult with an LD

It has always been my dream to teach. When I was diagnosed with a learning disability, I thought I would have to give up my dream as I felt it meant I was not smart enough. Others also bought into this stigma surrounding learning disabilities, which affected my self-esteem even more. I was not doing well in school at this point, often avoiding work or anything challenging due to my fear of failing and being thought of as dumb. The only areas I excelled in and genuinely enjoyed were math and science, though my language skills limited my growth in these areas. In Grade 4, my Principal recognized my potential, and pushed for me to be accepted into the Individual Support and Assessment (ISA) program. With the support of many other teachers, technological assistance, and the opportunity to flourish in my areas of strength, my confidence in my abilities started to grow. This confidence spilled over into other subject areas and my personal life. In elementary school, I would not tell anyone about my LD, and hated it being mentioned. At the beginning of high school, I would share this information with my friends, but that was it. My family worked so hard to help me realize that having this diagnosis is nothing to be ashamed of, and one that truly makes me who I am. Having known about my diagnosis has helped me to work hard to show others that I can in fact learn and work towards my dreams. Now I am always thrilled to tell people that I have a learning disability, was an honours student, won awards for top marks (in math, science, and computer courses) and have completed my B.Sc. The fact that I have a learning disability still shocks people. In Grade 12, I was trying to decide what I should be. Many different jobs came to mind with serious consideration; engineer, marine biologist, geneticist. None of these areas would have ever seemed possible to my 9-year-old self, but there I was, considering them and many more. But teaching was always my dream, and after all I went through, I really wanted to be that teacher who supported and pushed others like me to their full potential. Now I am at UOIT starting my first year in the Faculty of Education. A learning disability should not limit anyone. With the right support and the opportunity to find their special niche, anyone can be successful.

Parent of a young adult with Autism

When our son was first diagnosed with autism, talking to him about having that diagnosis certainly wasn't the first thing on my mind. He was almost 4 years old when he was diagnosed and it took time to absorb what the diagnosis meant and how to make sure we were doing everything in our power to find him the best resources to help him grow and thrive in a world where the majority of children his age were not autistic.

Prior to my son's diagnosis, I had a very limited understanding of what autism was and thought of it as an illness or a disorder. Through learning more about autism, I began to reframe my concept and saw it more as an atypical way of learning and interacting with the world. This became very important as I began thinking about how to talk with my son about autism. Although he never spontaneously asked questions about the different therapists that worked with him or the extra help he had at school I knew that he could tell there were differences between he and the other children in his class. I knew that I would have to fight my natural inclination to protect and shield him and focus more on giving him the confidence and tools to cope with this style of learning and communicating with the world. I also knew that in order to do this, I needed to gently and honestly talk to him about his diagnosis. I started by having very short and simple conversations with him about how people learn. I didn't shy away from using the word autism and I never presented it as a disorder but as something you are born with that makes you learn and communicate in a way different from many other people. I wanted to normalize it as one style of learning and communicating, even though it wasn't the most common style. We talked about how we were all different in our family in how we learned and we discussed that there were good things and difficult things no matter how you learned or communicated. We talked about how having autism helped with his amazing memory and martial arts skills but made participating in class and group sports more difficult for him than others.

I have never regretted my decision to be honest with my son and help him to understand his strengths and challenges as he interacts with his world. I genuinely believe that it helped him to become more confident and achieve things I never dreamt were possible when he was first diagnosed. He has taught me so much more than I could ever teach him and I'll never be able to truly express the depth of my admiration and love for him.

Preface

The explanation of the diagnosis is a complex and time sensitive process that cannot be completed in one or two sessions. For some children, it may take weeks, or even months, before an actual label of the diagnosis is provided. The overall process should be positive, feel safe, and build on your child's strengths and needs. To help make the information more meaningful, it is essential that your child is allowed time to understand and process the information provided at each step. Your child will be the guide for when they are ready to move on to the next step.

When explaining a diagnosis, your child may become angry or resentful. This is a natural part of the process. Don't give up or stop! At this stage, it is important to validate how they are feeling, reassure them that you are there to support them, and that you are on this journey together.

Overview of this Resource Guide:

The suggestions and examples provided are for reference only. It is essential that parents/guardians, school teams and other professionals work collaboratively with this process and to individualize each session to meet the needs of an individual child.

All children have their own unique set of learning strengths and needs. During this process, it is as important to identify an individual's strengths as it is to determine his or her needs. Many factors, including physical, intellectual, educational, cultural, emotional and social skills can influence an individual's ability to learn. Understanding and noting an individual's learning profile can aid in the teaching process which is critical to a child's learning.

Adapted from: The Ontario Unit Planner: Special Education Companion © Queen's Printer for Ontario, 2002.

Before You Begin

For many parents, deciding when and why to tell their child about their diagnosis can be a very emotional experience, and one which both parents may not always agree upon. When a child is first diagnosed, parents will often face a range of emotions that may be difficult to understand. Finding the support parents may require dealing with this new information is not always easy. It is essential that both parents have an opportunity to fully accept and understand their child's diagnosis themselves prior to beginning the process of explaining their child's diagnosis to the child. Therefore, there must be a level of agreement and support between parents when deciding to tell their child about their diagnosis.

Why parents decide to tell?

Many parents decide to tell their child about their diagnosis for them to feel supported and understand what is happening on a day to day basis. Explaining the diagnosis can help your child with self-advocacy, respect, and self-acceptance by lowering the risk of depression and anxiety as your child learns to cope and accept themselves while learning accurate information. It is important to teach your child that a diagnosis is nothing to be ashamed about, as every person deals with challenges in their lifetime that appear in different forms such as family, social, career, health, etc. A diagnosis does not define who we are, but rather provides us with information regarding areas of challenge and/or difficulty. Knowledge is a powerful tool that allows us to set goals, face obstacles, and utilize tools and strategies to navigate life. Without this understanding of self, children may be left wondering why they feel, look, or act a certain way, and question why certain things are more difficult for them to deal with in comparison to others. By beginning the process of explaining a diagnosis to a child, you are being proactive in your approach and working towards setting your child up for success in the future.

Why parents may not tell?

Some parents may decide not to tell their child about the diagnosis. This is a personal choice, and many factors may contribute to this decision. Some of these may include:

☐ age of child,
☐ cognitive understanding of child,
☐ recent diagnosis,

☐ lack of acceptance from peers and community, and
☐ one or both parents are still going through the acceptance stage themselves.

Other factors parents may consider justifying refraining from explaining the diagnosis is the fear that their child may not understand, get angry or become depressed, use the diagnosis as an excuse, or the chance they will be socially isolated by their peers. It is important to note that many of these factors may arise whether or not a child is told about their diagnosis. Many children may attempt to research on their own, find answers to questions they have, and may receive information that is not necessarily accurate, which can then lead to further anger, confusion and sometimes depression or anxiety.

When to *tell?*

As parents, you will need to work together to decide when the appropriate time is to explain the diagnosis to your child. There is no exact age or time that is correct for all families, and there are several factors that should be considered before you begin this process. These influences may include:

☐ a child's age,
☐ abilities,
☐ cognitive understanding, and
☐ social awareness.

If your child is very young, he or she may not fully comprehend what a diagnosis means, which can lead to confusion, and/or your child disclosing this information to others inappropriately or unnecessarily. A good way to test if your child is ready to be told about their diagnosis is by telling them something that is considered private, like a "fake" code to the garage door, and explaining to them that this is private information that cannot be shared with others. Then, have someone ask your child the code to their garage door. If your child shares this information, they may not be ready to understand the concept of private versus public information, and perhaps may not be ready to hear about their own diagnosis. The early steps of the process can begin but your child may not be ready for full disclosure of the information regarding their diagnosis.

Waiting to tell your child about his or her diagnosis at a much older age can also be problematic. Your child may have already begun to conceive that they are different from their peers, and thus may draw incorrect conclusions to explain these differences. This premature self-awareness can lead to a child becoming overly sensitive, confused, having lower self-esteem, withdrawing from others and sometimes even depression or anxiety. Your child may begin to ask questions like: "What is wrong with me?", "Why don't I have friends?", "Why am I different from her?" or "Why is this so hard for me?" As parents, you will want to watch for these types of questions as they may indicate that your child requires accurate information regarding their diagnosis. It is important to note that not all children will ask questions, though they may have similar thoughts that they have not expressed.

Explaining a child's diagnosis can be overwhelming, and many parents feel that they are not prepared or equipped with the necessary information. Some families may decide to have another family member or professional (e.g. a teacher, social worker, counsellor, therapist, psychologist etc.) begin the process. As parents, you will need to decide the best option for your child and your family. This guide will help take you through the steps so you, a family member or a professional can begin this process.

It is essential to keep in mind that this process should not be rushed. Let your child guide you through the sessions, as this process may take several weeks or months. It is important to remember that though your child may not be completely ready to be told about their diagnosis, you can still begin this process, as there are benefits to all children understanding concepts such as similarities/differences, and strengths/challenges. As you go through the sessions, you may notice that your child has some level of understanding of the content. This degree of understanding is positive, however, do not be tempted to skip sessions. It is always a good idea to review a session to ensure full comprehension. Ideally, you want to begin this process before your child expresses curiosity regarding differences they may observe in themselves in relation to their peers. Remember, children will often think of these things BEFORE they become vocal about their thoughts. You may want to investigate as to whether your child is asking questions about their differences to other figures in their life, such as siblings, teachers, coaches etc. If so, write down the questions they have asked others so that you may refer to them later in the sessions.

Another crucial step in the process of explaining a diagnosis to a child is to identify your child's learning style before you begin this process. Knowing your child's learning strengths will help guide you through the sessions with your child to help them best process the concepts and enhance their overall learning. Asking guiding questions throughout each session will help to ensure your child's comprehension of the main concepts of each discussion. Some critical thinking questions you may want to consider asking your child are:

☐ Why is this important?
☐ What does this mean for you?
☐ How can this help you?

These sessions are meant to act as a guideline. It is important to tailor these learning sessions according to the strengths and needs of your child. Ready to begin? Yes, you are!

Session 1: Identifying Your Child's Learning Style

Objective:

The aim of the first session is to help identify your child's learning style so that you can present the information that is in each section to best maximize a child's learning potential.

Materials:

- ☐ Paper
- ☐ Markers/Pencil
- ☐ Learning Styles Worksheet

Guidelines:

Step 1: Check off the statements that best represent your child. If you are unsure what to check off, then observe your child, ask other people or professionals who interact with your child or simply ask your child what they think best describes them.

Step 2: Add up the checkmarks in each section. Whatever section has the most checkmarks will indicate what learning style your child has an aptitude for.

It is important to remember that there is no objectively correct learning style and each style has different advantages. Knowing your child's learning style and working alongside your child's learning advantages will help them to learn the concepts more efficiently.

When engaging in the following activities with your child, you may ask yourself: "Should I use visuals, role play or discuss the activities?" When you can identify your child's learning style, you can use the methods that work best for them or perhaps a combination of methods, if that's what their profile reveals. Most people are not strictly confined to one learning style; however, there usually is one learning style that is prominent among the others.

Helpful Hint:
You may want to complete this activity on yourself or another family member to show your child that everyone learns in different ways.

Learning Styles Worksheet

Everyone learns new information in different ways. Check off (√) any of the items below that are true for you.

A:
- I can watch what people are doing.
- I prefer to use visuals such as graphic organizer, maps, or checklists.
- I like when a teacher uses charts, graphs, diagrams, handouts and projectors.
- I like creating and viewing visual images.
- When I need to assemble something, I follow the written instructions or a diagram provided.

B:
- Someone reads/explains things to me.
- I put things into a rhyme (e.g., song or pattern).
- When I need to assemble something, I like to have someone talk me through it.
- I like it when a teacher lectures, uses guest speakers and allows for discussion.
- The best way for me to recall an event would be through retelling the event out loud.
- The best way for me to receive directions would be to listen to the directions.

C:
- I can make things with my hands.
- When I forget how to spell a word, I write down different ways to spell the word.
- When I need to assemble something, I like to try to figure it out by physically manipulating the item through trial and error.
- I like it when teachers allow students to actively practice, demonstrate or role play.
- The best way for me to recall an event would be through acting it out.

Add up the sum of checkmarks in each column.

A – If you have the highest sum of checkmarks in the A. column, then you are more likely a visual learner.
B - If you have the highest sum of checkmarks in the B. column, then you are more likely an auditory learner.
C - If you have the highest sum of checkmarks in the C. column, then you are more likely a kinesthetic learner.

The 3 Key Learning Styles:

Visual Learners:

- ☐ Prefer to see what they are learning
- ☐ Think in pictures
- ☐ Enjoy looking at books and pictures
- ☐ Use maps, illustrations, charts, diagrams etc.
- ☐ Learn through visual instructions (words, pictures, signs etc.) and demonstration

Auditory Learners:

- ☐ Prefer to hear and talk about what they are learning
- ☐ Enjoy talking to others, music and story telling
- ☐ Learn by someone talking them through the steps

Kinesthetic Learners:

- ☐ Prefer to touch and physically manipulate what they are learning
- ☐ Gesture when speaking
- ☐ Enjoy hands on activities (touching and exploring objects) and physical activities
- ☐ Fidget and need movement
- ☐ Learn best by physically doing an activity

Adapted from: http://www.schoolonwheels.org/pdfs/3121/Learning-Styles.pdf,
http://www.georgebrown.ca/current_students/counselling/learning_styles.pdf,
www.georgebrown.ca/peerconnect/learning_styles.pdf

Session 2: Understanding Relationships

Objective:

The aim of this session is to help your child recognize that there are different types of people in their life, and that certain information and/or topics can be shared with certain people.

Materials:

- Coloured construction paper
- Picture of your child
- Photographs of different people (e.g., familiar and strangers)
- Paper
- Markers
- Tape or glue
- Sample Attributes and Conversational Topics

Guidelines:

Step 1: Place six or more pieces of coloured construction paper out in front of your child (note: have your child pick which colour of paper they would like to use to represent each category of relationships). Each coloured piece of paper is to be labelled to represent each classification of people (1. Child, 2. Family – mom, dad, siblings, grandparents etc. 3. Friends – classmates and play dates. 4. Community Helpers – police, teachers, dentist, doctor etc. 5. Acquaintances/People you don't know that well – students in other classes, mailman, garbage man etc. and 6. Absolute strangers). Note: you can always individualize the classification further. For example, after the category of the child, you may have mom and dad, or this section may contain only mom. Ensure that the category of people is individualized to your child and their social contacts. If your child demonstrates difficulty with identifying different colours, you may choose to alter this activity by simply numbering each category, using shapes, or even incorporating something related to their personal interests. For example, if your child enjoys baseball, they can be the pitcher, the team members are the friends, the coaches are the family, the people in the stand are the acquaintances etc.

Child	Family	Friends	Community	Acquaintances	Strangers

Step 2: Give your child a piece of paper with a name on it (e.g., "Aunt Thelma"), and ask your child to identify (name, point to, or place the paper with the name on top of the corresponding section) which category this person belongs to. You can also show your child pictures of people they know, and have them name the person and identify the category to which that person belongs. For the Community Helper and Stranger category, you can use cut out pictures from magazines and teach your child to say, "That's a police officer," or "I don't know who that is," or "That's a stranger." Repeat this step for every classification of people.

Step 3: Write down a list of different attributes on a piece of paper that an individual in a certain category will relate to, and have your child match these attributes to the corresponding category. After they can do this without any assistance, ask your child to define the roles each category encompasses, or identify the section in which an individual would belong. Sample attributes and conversational topics have been included for you in this section. It is important to consider the family's social, cultural, and religious beliefs when deciding which information will be paired to each category.

Step 4: At this stage, you are helping your child understand what types of information or topics they can share with others. For example, any information or topic of conversation that are appropriate for friends, community helpers, acquaintances and strangers can also be shared with family members. However, it is important to explain to your child that though you may tell family members certain information, that information may not be appropriate to share with the people in the categories above them. This is a great opportunity to review the concept of what is private versus public. For example, you may tell a friend and family member what movie you saw on the weekend, but you may only tell a family member personal information about yourself.

Sample Attributes and Conversational Topics:

I.   Child

II. Family:

  ☐ someone who is related to me
  ☐ someone that lives with me
  ☐ someone I go on vacation with
  ☐ someone who has the same last name as me

☐ I can tell them personal information about myself (example: my phone number, my address etc.)

☐ I can tell them about my health

III. Friends:

☐ children who live on my street

☐ children who are in my class or a different class

☐ children who I see in my afterschool daycare

☐ children I see during my extra-curricular activities (e.g. soccer, karate, robotics, chess club)

☐ children who come over to my house to play

☐ children who I play with during recess

☐ I can tell them what I ate for dinner

☐ I can tell them about my vacation

☐ I can tell them about my favourite games/hobbies

☐ I can tell them about my likes and dislikes

☐ I may tell some of them my phone number and address

IV. Community Helpers:

☐ can include my teachers, doctors, police officers, fire fighters etc.

☐ people to go to if I need help

☐ people to talk to if I am lost

☐ people to tell if I get hurt

☐ people who work in the community

☐ I can tell them my name

☐ I can tell them my phone number or address if I am lost

☐ I may tell some about my health (e.g. doctor/nurse, dentist)

V. Acquaintances:

☐ people I don't know that well

☐ someone I may have played with one or two times

☐ someone I can say "Hi" to

☐ people that I have seen my parents talk to, but I don't know them

☐ my parents' friends

☐ I may know their name, but nothing else about them

    ☐ someone who goes to my school, but is not in my class
    ☐ a friend of my friend
    ☐ I can smile
    ☐ If I have seen them many times before, I may tell them my name
    ☐ I can talk about the weather or current events (e.g. public information)

VI. Absolute Strangers:

    ☐ someone I have never seen before
    ☐ people I may have seen before, but never talk to
    ☐ I can appear friendly and smile

Helpful Hint:
If your child is not able to read, then complete this session using pictures of each classification of people.

Adapted from: McAfee, J. (2002). Navigating the Social World & Taubman, M. et al. (2011). Crafting Connections.

Session 3: Identifying Talents and Strengths

Objective:

    The primary aim of this session is to help your child understand that they have many talents and strengths and to help build their self-esteem by speaking about the things they can do well.

Materials:

- ☐ "My" Talents and Strengths Checklist
- ☐ "_____" Talents and Strengths Checklist
- ☐ Talents and Strengths Comparison Sheet
- ☐ Paper
- ☐ Pencil
- ☐ Recording system

Guidelines:

Step 1: Begin this session when you and your child are in a quiet place. You may decide to do this activity alone or with a partner. If you decide to involve another person in this process, then the person should be someone with whom your child feels comfortable and someone they can trust.

Step 2: Ask your child to tell you all about what they believe are their talents and strengths. Write them down on a piece of paper or you can use the "My" Talents and Strengths Checklist. At first, your child may have difficulty thinking of strengths that they believe are talents. Prompt your child by suggesting traits that you believe are positive, or activities and hobbies you have seen them enjoy doing. If your child prefers, they can always draw a picture of what they believe to be their talents and strengths.

Step 3: After your child has identified their own talents and strengths, use the "_____" Talents and Strengths Checklist to have them interview another person to find out about their talents and strengths. You may need to assist with prompts or adapt this activity if your child has difficulty with reading, spelling etc. An example of great idea to adapt this activity to your child's individual needs is for them to use an audio or video recording system to tape others' responses for the "_____" Talents and Strengths Checklist, or perhaps even draw a picture.

Step 4: Once both checklists are completed, fill out the Talents and Strengths Comparison sheet and point out any similarities and differences between them and the person they interviewed. Once this is completed, you may have a further conversation about what makes each of them unique and special. It is important to stress that every person is different and that we all have things that we are good at doing, and special qualities that makes us all important. Depending on the age of your child, you may want to consider reading the book *"I'm Like You, You're Like Me: A Book About Understanding and Appreciating Each Other"* by Cindy Gainer.

Helpful Hint:
Find out your child's talents and strengths by talking to others who know or work with them, including teachers, other family members (e.g. siblings), therapists, friends etc. You may also have your child survey more than one person to allow them to learn more about the talents and strengths of others.

My Talents and Strengths

Everyone has talents and strengths. My talents and strengths are activities that I feel that I am good at doing and enjoy.

Check off (√) any of the items below that are your talents and strengths.

- o Computers
- o Math
- o Writing stories or poetry
- o Reading
- o Drawing/painting
- o Sports
- o Building/constructing things
- o Video games
- o Photography
- o Dancing
- o Singing
- o Puzzles
- o Cooking
- o Playing an instrument
- o Remembering people's names
- o Knowing facts about _____

List some of your other talents and strengths that are not listed above:

_____

_____

_____

Adapted from: Attwood, T. (2004), Exploring Feelings: Cognitive Behaviour Therapy to Manage *Anger*

"_____" Talents and Strengths

     Everyone has talents and strengths. Ask someone you know (maybe a family member or a friend) about their talents and strengths.

Check off (√) any of the items below that are talents and strengths for:

_____.
  Write name above

- o Computers
- o Math
- o Writing stories or poetry
- o Reading
- o Drawing/painting
- o Sports
- o Building/constructing things
- o Video games
- o Photography
- o Dancing
- o Singing
- o Puzzles
- o Cooking
- o Playing an instrument
- o Remembering people's names
- o Knowing facts about _____

List some other talents and strengths that are not mentioned above:

_____

_____

_____

Adapted from: Attwood, T. (2004), Exploring Feelings: Cognitive Behaviour Therapy to Manage *Anger*

Talents and Strengths Comparison Sheet

Similarities	Differences

Session 4: Celebrating Differences

Objective:

The primary aim of this session is to help your child understand that every person has traits that make us different from one another, and to accept these differences, as these qualities make every person unique and should be celebrated.

Materials:

- ☐ Paper and pencil
- ☐ Talents and Strengths Checklists (from session 2)
- ☐ Talents and Strengths Comparison Sheet (from session 2)
- ☐ Visible/Invisible Differences Worksheet
- ☐ My Sensory Checklist
- ☐ Family/Friends Comparison Worksheet
- ☐ Sample Social Narrative

Guidelines:

Step 1: Explain to your child that every person is different, and that being different is okay. Explain that some differences are visible (i.e. we can see them). Visible differences are things we can see by looking at another person (e.g. gender, hair colour, eye colour, size, etc.). Then, explain that some other things that make us different are "invisible" (i.e. we cannot see them). Invisible differences are things about the person that we cannot see (e.g. what someone likes to eat, their talents or their interests). Explain to your child that we all have visible and invisible differences. Use the *Visible/Invisible Differences Worksheet* to write down your child's responses or have them draw a picture.

Step 2: Review the five senses with your child, and explain that our bodies and the environment send our brains information through our senses. This information is processed and organized so that we can feel comfortable and secure, and that we can respond appropriately to situations and environmental demands. Explain to your child that just like visible and invisible differences, our senses may interpret information differently than others. Using the *My Sensory Checklist*, have your child complete their own sensory profile. Once completed, have them use the *Sensory Comparison worksheet* and compare their answers to a family member's or a friend's sensory profile. Use this opportunity to stress the importance of being unique and the celebration of the special qualities that define us.

Step 3: Ask your child what the word "unique' means. Write their response on a piece of paper. Explain that no two people are exactly the same because of their talents, strengths, interests, invisible and visible differences. As a result of these specific qualities, each and every one of us is different and unique. Being different is okay! We are all important! Using the *Family/Friends Comparison worksheet*, emphasize their own uniqueness in comparison to other family members and friends. For example, how would you feel if all your friends or family members had the same birthday as you?

- ☐ You may NOT feel unique or special
- ☐ You may have to share a party
- ☐ You may have to share a cake
- ☐ You may not get as many presents

Think of other questions your child can ask family members or friends and compare the similarities and differences. Sample questions may include:

- ☐ When is your birthday?
- ☐ Do you have any siblings?
- ☐ What grade are you in?
- ☐ What radio stations do you listen to?
- ☐ Do have any pets?
- ☐ Do you know how to ice skate?
- ☐ What is your favourite movie or TV show?
- ☐ What type of sports do you play?
- ☐ What is your favourite food to eat for dinner?
- ☐ What is your favourite restaurant?

Once this session is completed, you may choose to write a social narrative with your child that describes their own unique differences, and that implies that these differences are okay. This narrative can be an effective tool to use when your child is still learning to understand about the concept of "differences." Remember, when writing the narrative, use clear and concrete langue and visual supports when needed so that it is easy for your child to comprehend. It is also important to write the narrative in a way that focuses on the positive nature of different traits and describes what a person may think, feel and do.

Helpful Hint:
Ask your child to list similarities and differences of family members. You may have to show your child pictures of people they know to help them generate a list of differences they can see.

Visible and Invisible Differences Worksheet

Visible	Invisible
Examples: - Hair colour	Examples: What someone likes to eat

My Sensory Checklist

Below is a list of items that relate to our senses. Check off (√) the ones that are true for you.

Sense of Smell

We use our nose to smell things around us. There are some smells you may like, and there are certain smells that may bother you. Check off the smells you like and dislike. You can add some of your own that have not been listed.

Like	Don't Like
○ Perfume/Cologne	○ Perfume/Cologne
○ Coffee	○ Coffee
○ Milk	○ Milk
○ Shampoo	○ Shampoo
Other:	○ Other:

My Sensory Checklist

Sense of Taste

We use our mouth and tongue to taste things. There are some things you like to eat or drink because of the taste, but some tastes may bother you. Check off the tastes you like and dislike. You can add some of your own that have not been listed.

Like	Don't Like
o Cheese	o Cheese
o Chocolate	o Chocolate
o Sour foods	o Sour foods
o Spicy foods	o Spicy foods
Other:	Other:

My Sensory Checklist

Sense of Hearing

We use our ears to hear the different sounds around us. Some are loud and some are very quiet. There are some sounds that you like or that don't bother you or hurt your ears, but there are certain sounds that may bother you. Check off the sounds that don't bother you and the ones that bother or hurt your ears. You can add some of your own that have not been listed.

Don't Bother Me	Bother Me
o Fire Alarms	o Fire Alarms
o Loud music	o Loud music
o Clock ticking	o Clock ticking
o Busy school hallway	o Busy school hallway
o Baby crying	o Baby crying
o Sudden noises	o Sudden noises
o Chair/desk scrapping along the floor	o Chair/desk scrapping along the floor
o Someone eating	o Someone eating
Other:	Other:

My Sensory Checklist

Sense of Sight

Seeing is what we do with our eyes. There are some things that you like to look at but certain sights may bother your eyes. Check off the sights you like and don't like. You can add some of your own that have not been listed.

Like	Don't Like
o Bright lights	o Bright lights
o Things that spin	o Things that spin
o Things that are in patterns	o Things that are in patterns
Other:	Other:

My Sensory Checklist

Sense of Touch

The skin on our body can feel when something is touching it. Sometimes there are certain touches that feel good on your skin, but certain touches bother or may even hurt you. Check off the ones you like and don't like. You can add some of your own that have not been listed.

Don't Bother Me	Bother Me
○ Buttons on clothes	○ Buttons on clothes
○ Tight clothing	○ Tight clothing
○ Jeans	○ Jeans
○ The seam on a pair of socks	○ The seam on a pair of socks
○ Tags on clothing	○ Tags on clothing
○ Getting a hair cut	○ Getting a hair cut
○ Washing my hair	○ Washing my hair
○ Brushing/combing my hair	○ Brushing/combing my hair
Other:	Other:

SAMPLE Family/Friends Comparison Worksheet

In the table below, Melissa filled in the answers to these 3 questions and compared the similarities and differences of her peers.

1. What colour are your eyes?
2. Birth order – are you the: oldest, middle, youngest, or only child?
3. What month were you born in?

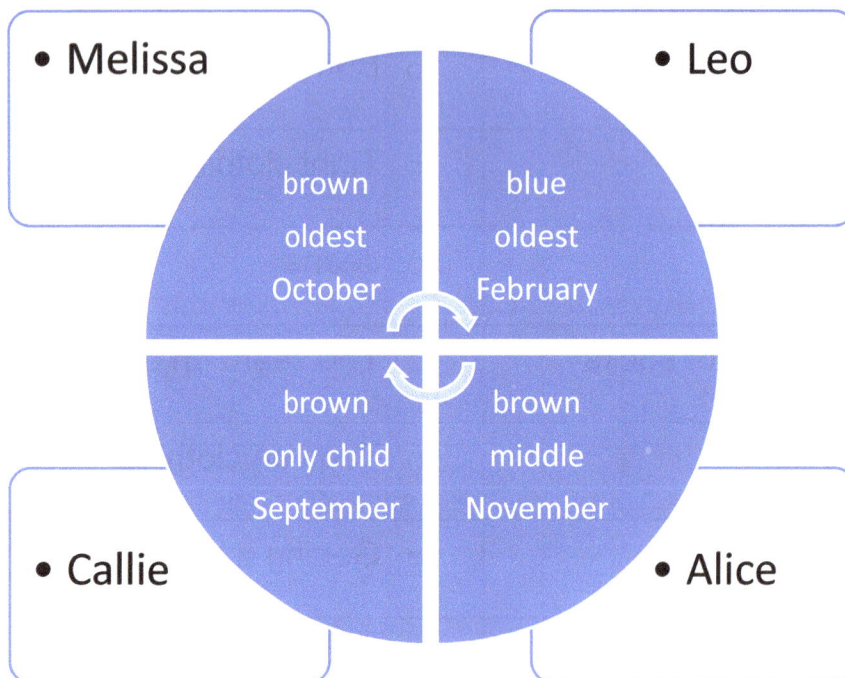

• Melissa	• Leo
brown oldest October	blue oldest February
brown only child September	brown middle November
• Callie	• Alice

How would you feel if all your friends/family members had the same birthday as you?

- o You may NOT feel unique or special
- o You may have to share a party
- o You may have to share a cake
- o You may not get as many presents

Think of other questions you can ask you family/friends and compare the similarities and differences.

Adapted from: Lynch, A., (2009), A Smart Girl's Guide to Understanding Her Family: Feelings, Fighting & Figuring It Out

Family/Friends Comparison Worksheet

In the chart below, fill in the answers to three or more questions and compare the similarities and differences of your family members and or friends. To reinforce this step, you may want to circle all the similarities. Be creative with the questions you come up with.

Sample Social Narrative

Celebrating Differences

My name is_____.

I like to do many things. I like to play on the computer and I like to do arts and crafts.

Sometimes other children might not like the things that I like. This is okay.

Sometimes I might not like what other children like to do. This is okay too.

It is okay that people like to do the same things or different things. This makes us all unique.

Being unique means we are all important.

It is okay to be different. We are all important.

We should remember to celebrate that we are all different.

Session 5: Understanding My Challenges

Objective:

   The primary aim of this session is to help your child understand that we all have things that may be challenging for us especially when it comes to learning or doing different things but sometimes what may be challenging at one point becomes an accomplishment.

Materials:

- ☐ Paper and pencil
- ☐ My Challenges Checklist
- ☐ "_____" Challenging Checklist
- ☐ Challenges Comparison Worksheet
- ☐ My Accomplishments Worksheet

Guidelines:

Step 1: Explain to your child that everyone learns new information. Sometimes learning new things can be easy and fast, while other times it may be difficult and may take a longer period of time. Ask your child to tell you all about some of the things they feel are challenging for them to do. Write them down on a piece of paper, or you can use the *My Challenges checklist*. Your child may have difficulty at first trying to come up with activities that they think are challenging; prompt your child by suggesting things that you believe might be more challenging for them. Remember, it is okay to find certain activities to be challenging. We all need to identify things we find difficult so that we can address them.

Step 2: After your child has identified their own challenges, use the "_____" *Challenging Checklist* and have them interview another person to find out about the things they find difficult

Step 3: Once both checklists are completed, fill out the *Challenges Comparison worksheet* and point out any similarities and differences between them and the person they interviewed. Once this is completed, you may have a further conversation about what makes each of them unique and special.

Step 4: It is important to discuss with your child that not all challenges will remain something that is difficult for them. At times, with the right support, time and practice their challenge may in fact become something that they enjoy doing and become a strength; these are called accomplishments. Fill in the *My Accomplishments Worksheet* with your child and discuss how they felt about the situation when it was a challenge and how they are feeling about it now (e.g. proud).

Helpful Hint:
Provide personal examples of things that you have felt were easy to learn and other things that were hard for you to learn or remain challenging for you, even as an adult. This will help reassure your child that everyone, including adults, has things that are difficult for them to do.

My Challenges

Everyone struggles to do certain things. These are called challenges. It is okay that we find some activities hard to do. My challenges are activities that I feel are difficult to complete.

Check off (√) any of the items below that you find difficult doing.

- o Computers
- o Math
- o Writing stories or poetry
- o Spelling
- o Reading
- o Drawing/painting
- o Sports
- o Building/constructing things
- o Video games
- o Puzzles
- o Cooking
- o Science
- o Playing an instrument
- o Remembering people's names
- o Knowing facts about _____

List some of your other talents and strengths that are not listed above:

_____

_____

_____

Adapted from: Attwood, T. (2004), Exploring Feelings: Cognitive Behaviour Therapy to Manage Anger

"_____" Challenges

Everyone struggles to do certain things. Ask someone you know (maybe a family member or a friend) about their challenges.

Check off (√) any of the items below that are difficult for _____.

Write name above

- o Computers
- o Math
- o Writing stories or poetry
- o Spelling
- o Reading
- o Drawing/painting
- o Sports
- o Building/constructing things
- o Video games
- o Puzzles
- o Cooking
- o Science
- o Playing an instrument
- o Remembering people's names
- o Knowing facts about _____

List some of your other talents and strengths that are not listed above:

_____

_____

_____

Adapted from: Attwood, T. (2004), Exploring Feelings: Cognitive Behaviour Therapy to Manage

Challenges Comparison Sheet

Similarities	Differences

My Accomplishments

What I found difficult. How I Felt About it.	What I did about it?	How I feel about it now?
Example: Reading- I felt frustrated when I was reading because I found it difficult.	Read books about my favourite things every night with my parents.	Something I enjoy doing now and like to read to others.

Step 6: Explaining the Diagnosis

Objective:

     The primary aim of this session is to help your child understand what their diagnosis is called and what it means for them.

Materials:

- ☐ Paper and pencil
- ☐ Relationship chart (e.g., child, family, friends, community helpers, acquaintance, strangers) – session 2
- ☐ What My Disability Means to Me Worksheet

Guidelines:

Step 1: Ask your child what the word disability means. They may tell you that they think the word means unable, or something that a person cannot do. Provide them with examples of other disabilities such as a person who is blind, deaf, or in a wheel chair.

- ☐ Then, ask your child if a person who is in a wheel chair is able to travel to a second floor of a building. If they say yes, ask how. If they are unable to provide an answer, explain to them that a person who uses a wheel chair may need to take an elevator, be carried, or use a ramp.
- ☐ Ask your child if a person who is blind can learn information from a book. If they say yes, ask how. If they are unable to provide an answer, explain to them that a person who is blind can find out information from a book by using special books that contain braille instead of written text, they may use audio books, or someone can read a book to them.

Step 2: Based on the examples above, explain that having a disability does not mean that you cannot do something; it just means that you may have to do it differently from someone else, and that is okay.

Step 3: Pick a time when things are more relaxed when you start to explain to your child that s/he has a disability called (_____). Let your child know that there are others who are diagnosed with this disability. It is important at this stage to be positive. Dr. Tony Attwood's book on Asperger's syndrome discusses how he sets the tone when delivering a diagnosis to a child. He introduces the diagnosis by announcing: "Congratulations! You have Asperger's syndrome!"

Make sure to focus on your child's positive traits (e.g. their talents and strengths) and emphasize those qualities when introducing your child's diagnosis.

Step 4: Depending on your child's disability, you may have to explain that you cannot see certain disabilities, because it affects the way the brain works, whereas other disabilities are more physical in nature (e.g. cerebral palsy). Your overall goal for this session is to reassure your child that having this difference does not mean that they can't learn, have fun, or have friends. You will have to explain to your child that a disability means that for certain aspects of learning, they may need to comprehend information in another way (e.g. it is easier if they see a picture, or read the information, rather than listening to someone talk.) or that it may take them longer to complete an activity, or participate in a different way (e.g. use a computer instead of writing).

Step 5: At this step, you want to inform your child that everyone, including those with a disability are unique and important. Being diagnosed with a disability is just another defining trait that makes them who they are. Discuss with your child that even though they have been diagnosed with a disability, they are still like everyone else in many ways (e.g. they go to school, should do homework, have talents and strengths, likes and dislikes, can learn to do new things, etc.). The important point to emphasize to your child is ensuring them NOT to be ashamed of having this disability. It is important to explain that it makes no difference to you as parents, as you love them no matter their diagnosis.

Step 6: It is critical to explain to your child that their disability it is neither their fault, or can be blamed on anyone else. In some circumstances, no one understands the origins of a disability. Scientists and researchers make continued efforts to understand the neurological and environmental causes of disabilities. A disability is not a disease, and disability is not contagious.

Step 7: Your child may begin to show resentment or even anger towards being diagnosed with a disability. Know that these harsh feelings are a normal part of the process of being diagnosed with a disability, and should be handled in a calm, and nurturing way. It is important to validate your child's feelings and help guide them through this process. It might be helpful to explain to your child that each person's brain works slightly differently from one another, and may cause them to act and think differently in some situations. This is a good time to refer to recent situations where your child may have reacted in a manner that was different from his/her peers.

Step 8: Sit with your child and research (e.g. use the internet or visit a library) famous individuals who may also have the same disability as your child. Explain to them that there are many happy and successful people who have the same diagnosis. A good resource to watch with your child is the video: "What do you see when you see me?" by Together for Autism and Autism Ontario. This video is about a group of kids who have been individually diagnosed with Autism, and are happy being who they are. You may also want to consider reaching out to a local agency related to your child's disability (e.g. Learning Disabilities Association, Autism Chapters, etc.) for other resources.

Step 9: Review the section on understanding relationships (session 2) to help guide your child through the process of recognizing the difference between private and public information. Discuss the topic of your child's diagnosis and decide which relationship categories are appropriate to share this information. It is important to consider the family's social, cultural, and religious beliefs when deciding who to share the diagnosis with.

Step 10: Now that you have given a name to the disability, have your child fill out the *What My Disability Means to Me* worksheet so they can keep a record of how the disability may impact them.

Example of who I can tell for a 6-year-old:

Child	Family Mom & Dad-yes Older Sibling- Yes Younger sibling- no	Friends- no	Community Helpers Teacher- yes Doctor- yes Bus Driver- no	Acquaintances- no	Strangers- no

Example of who I can tell for a 14-year-old:

Child	Family Mom & Dad-yes Older Sibling- Yes Younger sibling- maybe	Friends Close friends-yes Kids in class- no	Community Helpers Teacher- yes School counsellor- yes Doctor- yes	Acquaintances- no	Strangers- no

Remember that this part of the process may need to be reviewed for a few days before you move on to the next session. Let your child guide you through this process. Keep in mind that as your child grows and matures, they may encounter situations that prove to be a challenge for them. It is important to identify whether this is a result of their diagnosis or simply something that we may all experience at one time or another. The key is to provide your child with the necessary problem-solving tools to help them to deal with these difficult situations.

Helpful Hint:
This part of the process may need to be extended over a couple of days or even weeks. Once you have gone through the process of explaining the diagnosis to your child, you may want to seek additional counseling for your child.

Adapted from: McAfee, J. (2002). Navigating the Social World & Taubman, M. et al. (2011). Crafting Connections.

Sample- What My Disability Means to Me

My Disability is Called:	Autism Spectrum Disorder
Having This Disability May Mean…	**Having this Disability Does Not Mean…**
It is sometimes hard for me to say what I am thinking.	I can't learn ways to express how I am feeling so others will understand.
Makes it hard for me to make friends.	I will never have friends.
I have more meltdowns than my friends do.	I will not be able to learn how to control my feelings.

What My Disability Means to Me

My Disability is Called:	
Having This Disability May Mean…	Having this Disability Does Not Mean…

Session 7: Questions about the Diagnosis

Objective:

The primary aim of this session is to help answer any questions your child may have regarding their diagnosis.

Materials:

☐ Paper and pencil
☐ Questions I May Have Worksheet
☐ My "What if...? and "I can..." Worksheet

Guidelines:

Now that you have explained the diagnosis of _____, to your child, they may have questions that they would like _____ (write in the diagnosis) answered.

Step 1: Check off questions your child may have and write down the answers in the space provided. Your child may have other questions as well; write them down in the space provided on the *Questions I May Have* worksheet. If your child does not have any questions now, that is OK, as they may have questions later. You can help facilitate the discussion by asking them set questions. Please keep in mind you may not have the answers; however, this is an opportunity to research the information regarding your child's disability and their specific needs. It is also important to know that the questions and answers provided are for reference only. You may have your own set of answers based on your family experiences, culture and beliefs.

Step 2: This step may not be a formal step, but one that you begin when your child starts to express concerns or worries about the diagnosis. Your initial response may be to say, "don't worry" or perhaps try to distract your child from their worry. It is important to address their concerns, provide support and strategies to address these worries. When using these lists, remember your child's learning style. This may mean verbally discussing the worries or writing them down. In any case make sure to validate your child's worries. Have them place their worries into a "What if?" scenario and together address ways that they can work on solving their worries.

Helpful Hint:
It is normal for your child to have worries about their disability. Spend the time working with them and reassuring them that others too have similar feelings and together you can work on solving their worries.

Sample Questions and Answers

Questions	Answers
"Am I the only person who has this diagnosis?"	"No, there are many people who also have this too. Some even go to your school."
"Did I do something wrong to be like this?"	"This is not your fault. You were born this way, just like you were born with blue eyes. It is a part of who you are and we love you."
"Will people still like me?"	"Nothing has changed from last week until today. Your friends last week are still your friends today. You are still you and we love you just as much today as we did yesterday or last year.

Questions I May Have

- Am I the only person who has this diagnosis?

- Did I do something wrong to be like this?

- Will I always have this?

- Who can I tell about my diagnosis?

- Who else knows that I have this?

- How might this diagnosis impact me?

Questions I May Have

o What strategies can help me?

o What resources do I have available?

o Does this mean I'm not smart?

o Will people still like me?

o _____?

o _____?

o _____?

"What if...?" and "I can..."

Work with a teacher or parent to fill in this chart. Think about things you may be concerned or worried about and determine things you can try to do to help yourself.

"What if...?"	"I can..."
Example: My friends find out about my disability?	I can talk to my parents and ask them to help me think of something I can tell them.

Session 8: This is Me!

<u>Objective:</u>

The primary aim of this session is to help your child be proud of who they are.

<u>Materials:</u>

- ☐ This is Me! Worksheet
- ☐ Picture frame

<u>Guidelines:</u>

Step 1: Now that you have told your child about their disability, it is important to remind them that they are a person who has many likes, dislikes, talents and strengths and having this diagnosis is just another thing about them. Refer to previous handouts and worksheets to help them understand who they are. Complete the *This is Me! Worksheet* to help consolidate all the information you have collected.

Step 2: Have your child draw a picture/self-portrait that represents who they are. Hand your child a mirror, and have them explain some key features they can see (e.g. visible). By creating a self-portrait, children learn who they are, how they want to present themselves, what is important to them, or place a picture of themselves in the picture frame provided. If your child does not enjoy drawing you can always have them place a photo of themselves into the picture frame. Make sure to find a picture that truly captures their personality.

Helpful Hint:
Some children prefer not to draw. You can still make this an enjoyable activity by drawing for them and ask them to help you or provide feedback on your drawing.

This is Me!

Fill out the things below to remind yourself and others of who you are!

- My name is _____

- My birthday is _____

- My eye colour is _____

- My hair colour is _____

- I am _____years old

- My school is called _____

- My friends are _____

- My learning style is_____

- I am good at playing _____

- My talents are_____

- My challenges are _____

- My favourite food is_____

- Sometimes _____is hard for me to do

- I have _____sisters

- I have _____brothers

- I have accomplished _____

List other things you would want people to know about you.

Draw a picture (or place a photo) of yourself in the space below.

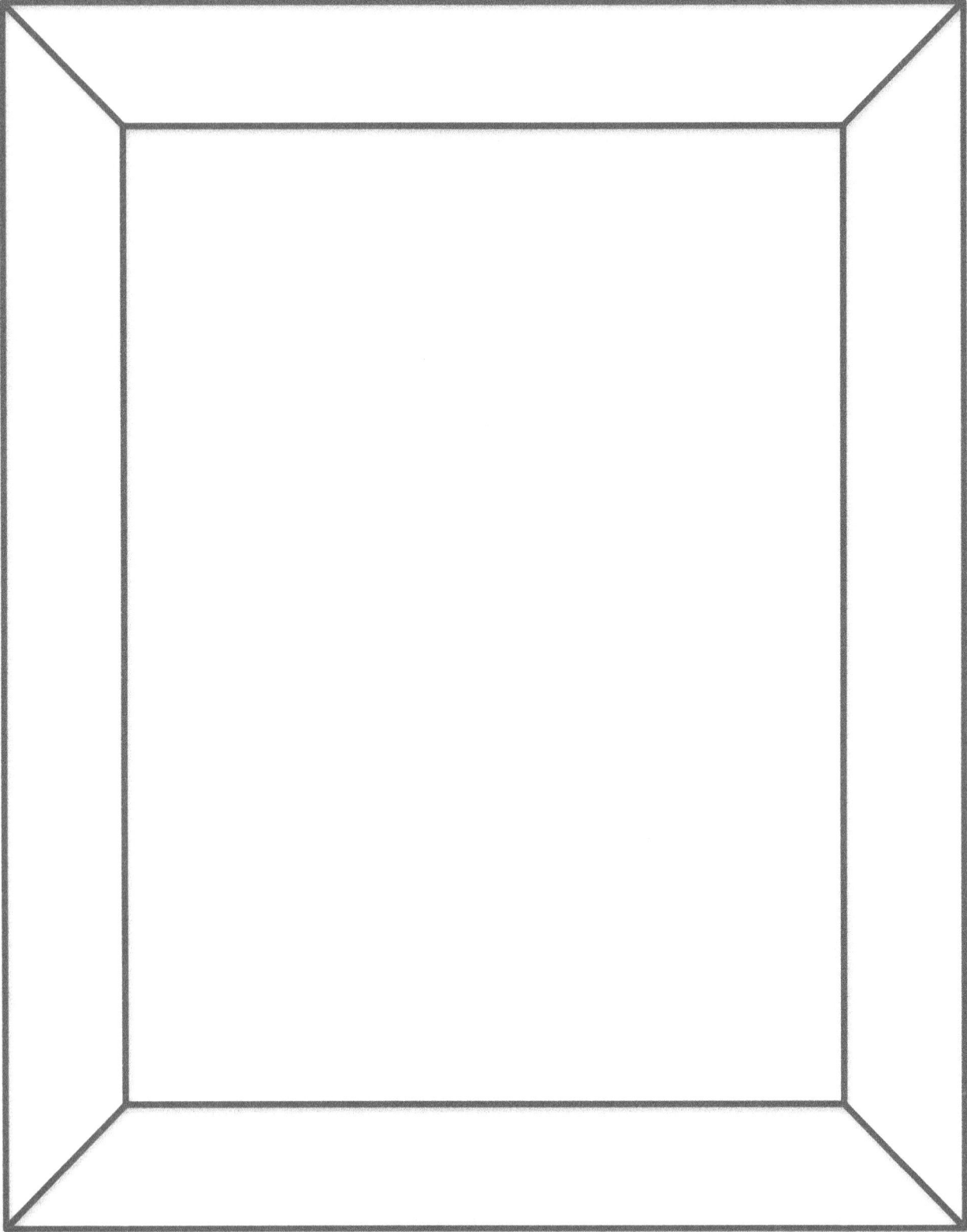

Session 9: My WHEEL of Support

Objective :

The primary aim of this session is to identify the people who may support your child, and how they may support your child after learning about their diagnosis. At times, your child may feel upset, worried, resentful, or perhaps even deny the fact that they have a diagnosis. This section will help you develop a WHEEL of support that you and your child can access when needed.

Materials:

Pencil
WHEEL of support diagram
Pictures and contact info of possible people of support

Guidelines:

Step 1:Brainstorm a list of people with your child who may be able to act as a source of support in various setting such as:

SCHOOL- teacher, principal, resource staff, guidance counsellor, friends etc.
COMMUNITY- priest, Rabbi, social worker, neighbor, doctor etc.
HOME- parents, sibling, grandparent, pet etc.

Step 2: List how these people may be a source of support.

Consider:

W – the WH questions your child may have (Why did this happen to me?
    Who else has this?)
H – the various sources of HELP your child may need
E – the various people who can provide EXPLANATIONS
E – the people who your child can share their EXPERIENCE with
L – the people who will provide opportunities for your child to LEARN coping skills

Adapted from: Criswell, P.K., (2015), Friends-Making them and keeping them.

In the diagram below, see a sample of people/pets that may provide you with support and how they may support you.

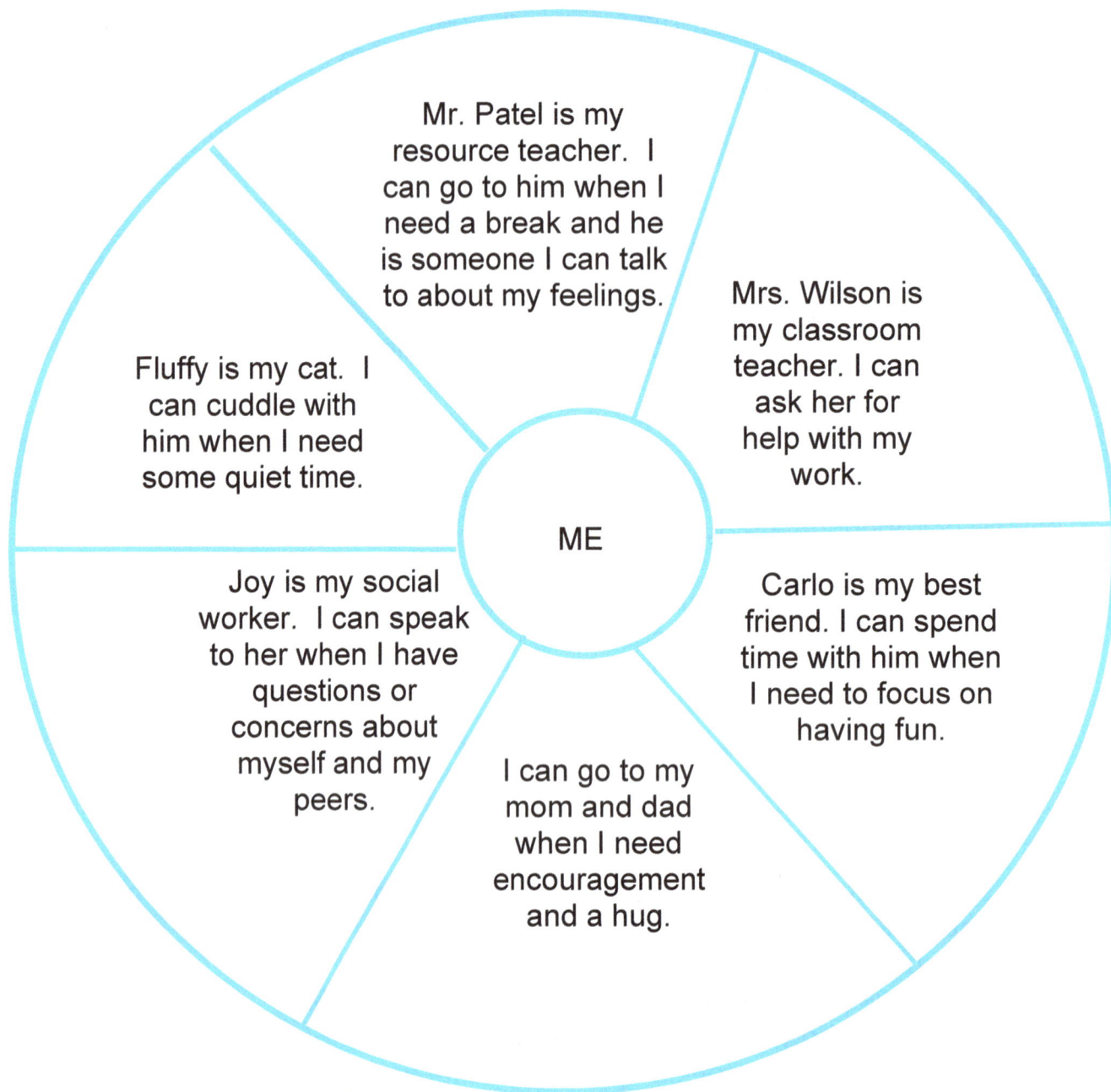

Mr. Patel is my resource teacher. I can go to him when I need a break and he is someone I can talk to about my feelings.

Mrs. Wilson is my classroom teacher. I can ask her for help with my work.

Fluffy is my cat. I can cuddle with him when I need some quiet time.

ME

Carlo is my best friend. I can spend time with him when I need to focus on having fun.

Joy is my social worker. I can speak to her when I have questions or concerns about myself and my peers.

I can go to my mom and dad when I need encouragement and a hug.

My WHEEL of Support

In the diagram below, add in people who can support you and how they can support you.

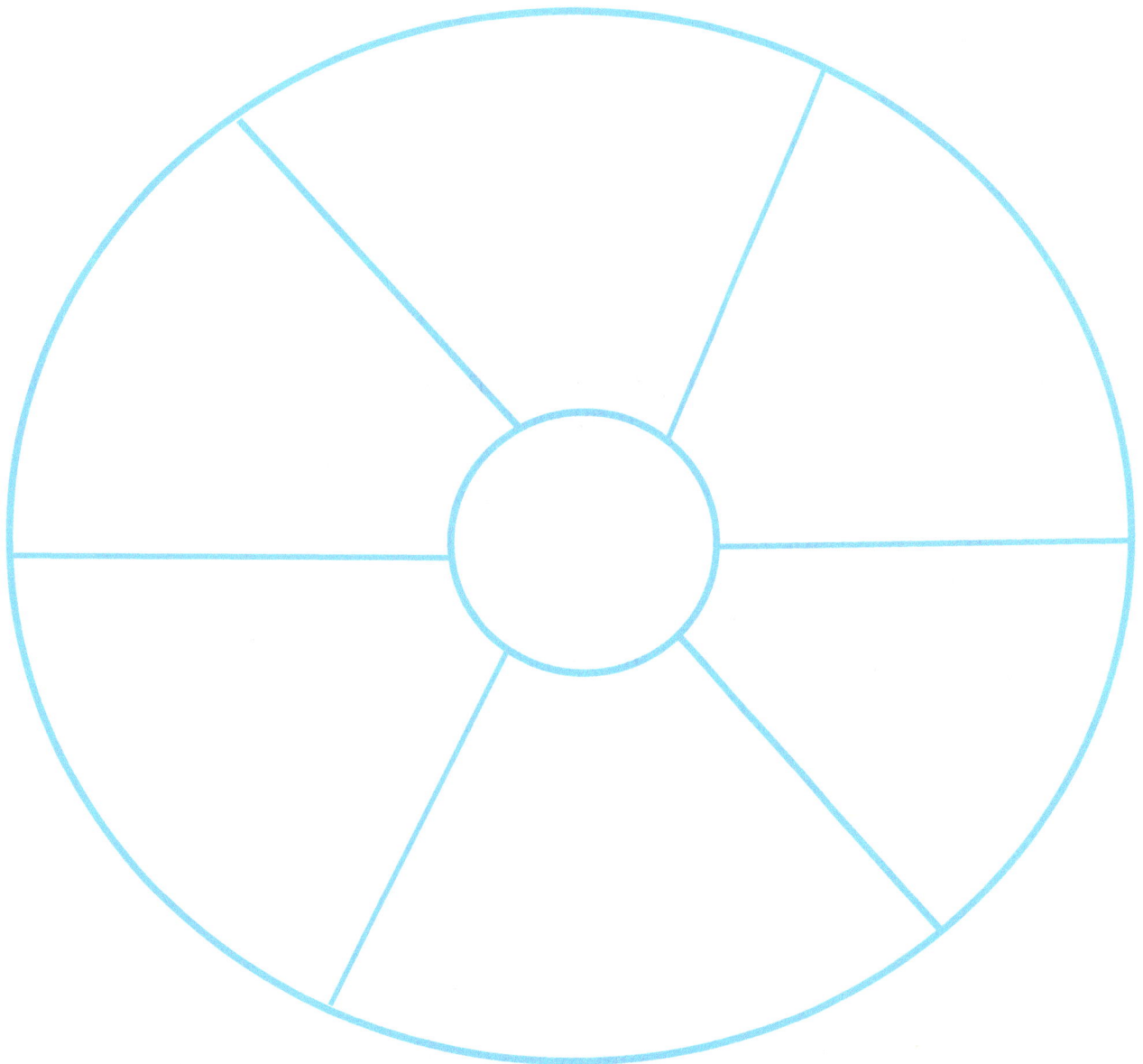

Helpful Hint:
You may decide to print and laminate this wheel and post it somewhere handy and visible to your child such as your child's room or in their agenda pocket.

Session 10: Self-Advocacy Cards

Objective:

The primary aim of this session is to help your child collect information they have learnt about themselves and their needs, and to place that information on paper in order to communicate their needs to educators.

Materials:

- ☐ Paper/pens
- ☐ Picture of child
- ☐ Advocacy Card Template

Guidelines:

Step 1: Sit down with your child and review the information from the previous sessions. Have your child write down all the things they would like their teachers to now about themselves. This may include things such as their interests as well as their learning style. Ask your child questions about how they learn best based on their learning style. Examples may include:
- ☐ prefer when they see teachers use visuals
- ☐ have questions repeated
- ☐ positive praise and feedback
- ☐ allowed extra time to do their work
- ☐ to complete work in a quiet area
- ☐ word dictionary
- ☐ highlighting key words
- ☐ fidget toys
- ☐ use of simplified language
- ☐ scribing
- ☐ use of technology

Step 2: Have your child write down all the things they find are challenging for them in a classroom environment. Examples may include:
- organization
- processing speed
- recall and memory
- reading fluency

- reading comprehension
- sustaining attention and focus
- confidence speaking in large groups
- recalling multiple step instructions
- note taking

Step 3: Some children may not know how to use the cards with their teachers so it is always a good idea to practice role playing with your child. Have your child act out how they will use these cards and communicate their needs to their educators. It is also suggested to arrange a meeting with the classroom teacher and discuss with them the purpose of the card. The goal of this activity is to empower your child so they can begin to advocate for themselves.

Note: some children may not want to have certain accommodations made in the classroom as they may fear others will think that they are different. This is a normal reaction from some children, and one that again allows you the opportunity to have those conversations that being different is okay. It might be a good idea to arrange a meeting with your child's classroom teacher and discuss the cards prior to your child introducing it to them. You might also want to suggest that the teacher have all the students in the class make self-advocacy cards.

Helpful Hint:
Some children prefer not to write, so you can create the self-advocacy card on a computer.

Adapted from: https://www.ldatschool.ca/self-advocacy/a-teachers-journey-with-student-self-advocacy/

Sample Advocacy Card

Picture of Child

My Strengths...What Helps Me	I Sometimes Have Difficulty with....
☐ Visual Learner – when teachers use graphic organizers and pictures ☐ Writing tests in a quite area ☐ Sitting close to the front of the class ☐ Drawing and sketching faces ☐ Working in small groups ☐ Encouragement and praise from teachers ☐ Highlighting key words	☐ Knowing the meaning of words ☐ Reading fluency ☐ Loud noises- I can be easily distracted ☐ Speaking in front of large groups ☐ Spelling ☐ Asking for help

Adapted from: https://www.ldatschool.ca/self-advocacy/a-teachers-journey-with-student-self-advocacy/

_____'s Advocacy Card

Picture of Child

My Strengths...What Helps Me	I Sometimes Have Difficulty with....

Session 11: Moving forward

The primary aim of this session is for you to continue to help your child and support them through this journey. Now that you have completed the process of explaining the diagnosis to your child, there may be additional supports that you and your child may require. Some of these supports may include:

☐ Keeping a journal (e.g. text or pictures). This is a healthy outlet when faced with overwhelming emotion. Keeping a journal allows your child to express themselves, while managing their mental health.

☐ Create a book together where my child can write a story showcasing a character that relates to them and what they are experiencing and hope to achieve.

☐ Read books about others with the same disability.

☐ Weekly family check-ins. This is a great opportunity to discuss the "highs" and lows" of the week and to check in to see how everyone is doing. It may seem difficult at first to remember to do this but it is a good idea to incorporate into a family ritual. For example, while driving in the car, or during meal time, or before bed.

☐ Seeking additional professional support. This may involve scheduling regular sessions with a psychologist, social worker, or therapist.

☐ Joining a local group/association related to the disability. This is a great opportunity to meet other families who are experiencing similar issues. When individuals meet, they can sometimes gain a better understanding of themselves and the world by interacting with others who also have the similar profiles. It helps parents and children realize that they are not alone. Joining a local group or association also allows you the opportunity to gain access to more resources and overall support for you and your child.

☐ Tracking personal accomplishments. When we keep a record of all the things we have accomplished it is a visual reminder that we can use to celebrate our "wins," use as motivation when things seem difficult, and help to build our overall confidence. This can be done by using a journal, or even creating an "Accomplishment wall."

Over time, you may have to revisit previous sessions; this is okay. As your child grows and adopts a perspective about themselves they may need to learn new ways to cope with the understanding of their disability and what it means for them. Consider the following questions to help address their understanding and acceptance:

- Do I need to seek support for my acceptance of my child's disability?
- Is my child able to articulate their strengths?
- Can my child name their disability and what it means for them?
- Does my child know who is in their life to support them?
- Does my child know anyone who also has the same diagnosis?
- Do I need to seek additional supports for my child?
- Have I explained the diagnosis to their sibling?

This guide has primarily focused on explaining the diagnosis to your child with a disability. Keep in mind that the same type of information that you provide to your child can also be used and shared with siblings. Just as you would consider the age and cognitive development of your child, the same is true for the child's siblings. Share information in a manner that they can process and comprehend. Just as you will need to continually support your child with the disability, you will also have to provide guidance for their siblings.

By explaining the diagnosis, you are beginning to set the stage for your child to understand, and accept who they are and that the disability is a part of them, it does not define them. The goal is to work towards building a confident individual who can self-advocate and perhaps even be an ambassador for others.

We wish you all the luck on this journey!

Janet and Francine

About the Authors

Janet Arnold, BA, RECE

Janet Arnold is a mother and advocate for her two boys. She has experienced what it is like to have a child with a disability, and has spent countless hours explaining the diagnosis to her own son.

Not only is Janet a mother, she is also a professional with over 20 years of experience working with children and youth with varying challenges, their families, and other professionals in clinical and educational settings in Ontario, Newfoundland, and Alberta. She is responsible for consulting, training, researching and developing resources on evidence-based and best practices in supporting positive development.

Janet is a Behaviour Consultant, HIGH 5® Trainer and an accredited Triple P Practitioner (Standard Stepping Stones). She is also actively involved in a variety of community working groups and is the Chair of the York Region Bullying Prevention Partnership, and holds professional memberships with the Learning Disabilities Association of York Region, the College of Early Childhood Educators (CECE), The Council for Exceptional Children as well as the Association of Early Childhood Educators Ontario (AECEO).

Francine McLeod, BSW, RSW

Francine McLeod is a Registered Social Worker, Behaviour Consultant, Certified Professional Coach, School Counselor and a mother of two girls. She has worked with children and youth with developmental challenges and social-emotional concerns, their families and the systems that support them since 1995.

Francine has taken her experience and knowledge of evidence-based and best practices of child development to provide on-going training, consultation, coaching, counseling and resource development to families, therapists, educators and other professionals.

Having worked in clinical and educational settings across Canada, she has a strong understanding of the importance of collaboration among families and professionals to ensure that children and youth are more fully included into the fabric of the community.

References

Aquilla, P, Sutton S., Yack, E. (1998). *Building Bridges through Sensory Integration.* Arlington, TX: Future Horizons

Attwood, T. (2004). *Exploring Feelings: Cognitive Behaviour Therapy to Manage Anger.* Arlington, TX: Future Horizons

Criswell, P.K., *(2015). Friends-Making them and keeping them.* Middleton, WI: American Girl Publishing

Dunn Buron, K. (2007). *A "5" could make me lose control.* Shawnee Mission, KS: Autism Asperger.

Faherty, C. (2000). *Asperger's...What does it mean to me?* Arlington, TX: Future Horizons

Gray, C. (1995). Social stories unlimited: Social stories and comic strip conversations. Jenison, MI: Jenison Public Schools.

Harris, S. (2003). *Siblings of Children with Autism.* Bethesda, MD: Woodbine House

Kaminsky, L. & Dewey, D. (2001). *Sibling relationships of children with autism.* Journal of Autism and Developmental Disorders, 31, 399-410.

Kranowitz, Carol. (2003). *The Out-of-Sync Child Has Fun. Activities for Kids with Sensory Integration Dysfunction.* New York: Penguin Putnam Inc.

Lynch, A., *(2009). A Smart Girl's Guide to Understanding Her Family: Feelings, Fighting & Figuring It Out.* Middleton, WI: American Girl Publishing

McAfee, J. (2002). *Navigating the social world.* Arlington, TX: Future Horizons.

Ministry of Education (2002). *The Ontario Unit Planner: Special Education Companion©* Queen's Printer for Ontario

Pritchard, A. (2014). *Ways of Learning. Learning theories and styles in the classroom.* New York, NY: Routledge

Taubman, A. et.al (2011). *Crafting Connections. Contemporary Applied Behavior Analysis* for Enriching the Social Lives of Persons with Autism Spectrum Disorder New York, NY: DRL Books Inc.

Website References

http://www.autismontario.com/

http://www.georgebrown.ca/current_students/counselling/learning_styles.pdf

http://www.georgebrown.ca/peerconnect/learning_styles.pdf

https://iancommunity.org/cs/articles/telling_a_child_about_his_asd

http://www.iidc.indiana.edu/irca/generalinfo/disabilityInfo.html

http://www.members.tripod.com/stevens_mom/id44.html

http://www.schoolonwheels.org/pdfs/3121/Learning-Styles.pdf

http://www.togetherforautism.ca/client/aso/TFA.nsf/web/Videos

www.ingramcontent.com/pod-product-compliance
Lightning Source LLC
Chambersburg PA
CBHW080602030426
42336CB00019B/3302